Common exception words

This book belongs to

....

Colour the star when you complete a page.
See how far you've come!

Author: Shelley Welsh

How to use this book

- Common exception words are words that your child will come across on a daily basis, but which do not follow the usual phonetic spelling rules that childen learn in primary school. This can make them more challenging to learn to read and spell than other words. This book will help to familiarise your child with these common exception words and develop their confidence in reading them and spelling them.

- The book has been written in a logical order, so start at the first page and work your way through. It starts with the common exception words that are taught in Year 1 and progresses to the common exception words that are taught in Year 2. From page 9 onwards, encourage your child to join the letters of the words if they know how.

- Find a quiet, comfortable place to work, away from distractions.

- Help with reading the instructions where necessary and ensure that your child understands what to do.

- Always end each activity before your child gets tired so that they will be eager to return to the book next time.

- Help and encourage your child to check their own answers as they complete each activity.

- Let your child return to their favourite pages once they have been completed. Talk about the activities they enjoyed and what they have learnt.

- Reward your child with plenty of praise and encouragement.

Special features of this book:

- **Progress chart:** when your child has completed a page, ask them to colour in the relevant star on the first page of the book. This will enable you to keep track of progress through the activities and help to motivate your child.

- **'Look, say, cover, write, check' method:** each page begins with your child being encouraged to familiarise themselves with the common exception words on that page. They are asked to say each one out loud and then cover it, write it and check it.

Published by Collins
An imprint of HarperCollins*Publishers* Ltd
The News Building
1 London Bridge Street
London SE1 9GF

HarperCollins*Publishers*
Macken House, 39/40 Mayor Street Upper,
Dublin 1, D01 C9W8, Ireland

© HarperCollins*Publishers* Ltd 2026

10 9 8 7 6 5 4 3 2 1

ISBN 978-0-00-877528-5

The author asserts the moral right to be identified as the author of this work.

All rights reserved. No part of this publication may be reproduced, stored in a retrieval system, or transmitted, in any form or by any means, electronic, mechanical, photocopying, recording or otherwise, without the prior permission of Collins.

Without limiting the exclusive rights of any author, contributor or the publisher of this publication, any unauthorised use of this publication to train generative artificial intelligence (AI) technologies is expressly prohibited. HarperCollins also exercise their rights under Article 4(3) of the Digital Single Market Directive 2019/790 and expressly reserve this publication from the text and data mining exception.

British Library Cataloguing in Publication Data

A Catalogue record for this publication is available from the British Library.

Author: Shelley Welsh
Publisher: Fiona McGlade
Editor: Katie Galloway
Cover design: Sarah Duxbury
Interior concept design: Ian Wrigley
Page layouts: QBS Learning and Sarah Duxbury
Production: Bethany Brohm
All images ©Shutterstock.com and
©HarperCollins*Publishers*
Printed in the UK

Contents

the, to, was, I, a	4
is, his, said, says	5
they, by, of, are	6
one, once, do, my	7
be, he, me, she, we	8
push, put, pull, full	9
you, your, no, go, so	10
there, where, our, has	11
here, were, school, today	12
house, ask, friend	13
love, come, some	14
child, children, again, because	15
both, cold, gold, hold, told, old	16
every, everybody, any, many	17
would, should, could	18
Christmas, most, only, sugar, sure	19
behind, find, kind, mind, wild, climb	20
hour, door, floor, poor	21
half, pass, grass, class	22
busy, after, path, bath	23
past, fast, last, plant	24
water, beautiful, pretty	25
break, steak, great	26
Mr, Mrs, parents, people	27
money, who, whole	28
move, improve, prove	29
clothes, father, even, eye	30
Answers	31

the, to, was, I, a

1 Colour the letters of the words below.

the to was I a

2 Look at each word below.

Say it out loud, then cover it, write it and check it.

the	to	was	I	a
___	___	___	_	_

3 Write the missing words in the sentences below.

__ am Sofia. __ go ____ school.

__ am Tom. __ have __ ball and _____ ball is red.

My old ball _____ blue.

is, his, said, says

1 Trace the letters of the words below.

is   his   said   says

2 Look at each word below.
Say it out loud, then cover it, write it and check it.

is	his	said	says
___	____	____	____

3 Find and circle the words **is**, **his**, **said** and **says** in the box below.

at	is	them	miss	in
him	that	on	the	his sad
said	says	fit	fin	finds

4 Write the missing words in the sentences below.

Dad ____ tired.

The girl _____ hello.

That is _____ ball.

I _____ goodbye.

they, by, of, are

1 Colour the letters of the words below.

they   by   of   are

2 Look at each word below.

Say it out loud, then cover it, write it and check it.

they	by	of	are
____	___	___	____

3 Find the word in each sentence that has been spelled incorrectly. Write the correct spelling on the line next to each.

Thay like dancing. _____

I brush my teeth bye myself. ____

I have a slice ov pizza. ___

We arr singing. ____

one, once, do, my

1 Trace the letters of the words below.

one   once   do   my

2 Look at each word below.

Say it out loud, then cover it, write it and check it.

one	once	do	my
___	_____	__	__

3 Find and colour the words hidden in the wordsearch.

g	e	k	y
o	n	e	d
o	b	a	o
n	x	v	q
c	m	m	y
e	q	a	z

one

do

my

once

4 Write the missing words in the sentences below.

Remember to use a capital letter at the beginning of a sentence.

_____ upon a time, a cat lived on a farm. "Where is ___ food?" he asked ____ day. "I can't ___ any hunting if I haven't had ___ food!"

7

be, he, me, she, we

1 Colour the letters of the words below.

be he me she we

2 Look at each word below.
Say it out loud, then cover it, write it and check it.

be	he	me	she	we
___	___	___	____	___

3 Say the words above out loud a few times. What do you notice?
They rhyme!
Circle the objects below that also rhyme with these words.

4 Write the missing words in the sentences below.
Remember to use a capital letter at the beginning of a sentence.

_____ likes ___ .   ____ eats apples.

____ read our books.   ____ careful!

push, put, pull, full

1 Trace the letters of the words below.

push   put   pull   full

2 Look at each word below.

Say it out loud, then cover it, write it and check it. Join up your letters if you know how.

push	put	pull	full
___	___	___	___

3 Write the missing words in the sentences below.

After my breakfast, I feel _____.

I _____ my bike up the hill.

We _____ the toys in the box.

My baby brother likes to _____ my hair.

4 Draw a line from each word on the left to a word on the right that has the same spelling apart from the first letter, but a different sound.

push	dull
pull	cut
put	gull
full	rush

you, your, no, go, so

1 Colour the letters of the words below.

you your no go so

2 Look at each word below.
Say it out loud, then cover it, write it and check it.

you	your	no	go	so
___	___	___	___	___

3 Colour the five words above that are hidden in the wordsearch.

y	g	e	k	y
o	o	n	o	y
u	z	b	a	o
r	s	o	v	u

4 Say the words **no**, **go** and **so** out loud. What do you notice?

They rhyme!

5 Write the missing word in each sentence below.
Underline another word in the sentence that rhymes with it.

There is ___ snow left in the garden!

Please can we ___ on the slow rides at the fair?

The temperature is low ___ wear your warm coat.

there, where, our, has

1 Trace the letters of the words below.

there where our has

2 Look at each word below.
Say it out loud, then cover it, write it and check it.

there	where	our	has
_____	_____	_____	_____

3 Circle the words in the box that rhyme with **there** and **where**.

chair   were   for   care   floor   here

their   fear   more   dear   dare   fair

4 Write the missing word in each sentence below. Underline another word in the sentence that rhymes with it.

Remember to use a capital letter at the beginning of a sentence.

We shall meet _____ friends in one hour.

_____ is the pear that Mum gave me?

Iris _____ as many crayons as I have.

_____ is the pair of socks I was looking for!

here, were, school, today

1 Trace the letters of the words below.

here were school today

2 Look at each word below.

Say it out loud, then cover it, write it and check it.

here	were	school	today
___	___	___	___

3 Write the missing words in the sentences below.

Remember to use a capital letter at the beginning of a sentence.

The book is over _____.

_____, after _____, we are watching a film

but yesterday, we _____ playing football.

4 Unscramble the jumbled words.

rewe	yadot	loocsh	ehre
___	___	___	___

house, ask, friend

1 Trace the letters of the words below.

house ask friend

2 Look at each word below.
Say it out loud, then cover it, write it and check it.

house	ask	friend
_____	_____	_____

3 Write the answers to the clues in the boxes.

A building you live in

Someone you care about

What you do when you want to know the answer to a question

4 Write one or more sentences using the words **house**, **ask** and **friend**.

love, come, some

1 Look at each word below.
Say it out loud, cover it, then write it. Check your spelling.

love	come	some
____	____	____

2 Find the five words in the passage below that have been spelled incorrectly. Write them correctly on the lines below.

I would luv sum ice cream. Would you like to cum with me to buy sum? I luv vanilla and strawberry.

____ ____ ____ ____ ____

3 Write the missing words in the poem below.
Remember to use a capital letter at the beginning of a sentence

Would you like to _____ with me

To see the sea and swim with me?

How I _____ to splash and run!

_____ day I hope

you'll _____ with me!

14

child, children, again, because

1 Look at each word below.
Say it out loud, cover it, then write it. Check your spelling.

child	children
_____	_____
again	because
_____	_____

2 Use the pictures to help you write the correct word: **child** or **children**.

 one _____    two _____

3 Look at this example showing you how to remember to spell the tricky word **because**. Talk with an adult about another way that might help you.

b big   **b**…
e elephants **e**…
c can   **c**…
a always   **a**…
u understand **u**…
s small   **s**…
e elephants **e**…

4 Find and colour the words hidden in the wordsearch.

x	u	p	r	b	e	c	a	u	s	e
d	b	a	g	a	i	n	p	r	e	b
f	c	h	i	l	d	q	a	f	g	z
c	h	i	l	d	r	e	n	l	v	y

15

both, cold, gold, hold, told, old

1 Look at each word below.

Say it out loud, cover it, then write it. Check your spelling.

both	cold	gold
___	___	___
hold	told	old
___	___	___

2 Write the missing words in the story below.

Remember to use a capital letter at the beginning of a sentence.

A little _____ man and a little _____ woman lived in a little _____ house. One day, the little old woman found a _____ coin. "_____ your hands out. I _____ you we would be rich!"

"Now we _____ have enough money for fire wood," he said. "We will never be _____ again!"

3 Use the clues to fill in the crossword.

Across
1. A precious metal
2. When there are two things

Down
3. The opposite to hot
4. Carry

every, everybody, any, many

1 Look at each word below.

Say it out loud, cover it, then write it. Check your spelling.

every	everybody
___	___
any	many
___	___

2 Circle the letter or letters in the words **any** and **many** that you think make them hard to spell.

Think of a way to help you remember how to spell these words. One example is:

I c**an** spell **an**y and m**an**y.

3 Say **every** and **everybody** out loud. Try to say each syllable clearly.

ev-**er**-**y**   **ev**-**er**-**y**-**bod**-**y**

4 Write the four words in the passage that have been spelled **incorrectly** on the lines below.

"So meny children are off sick today,"

said the teacher. "Evrybody listen!

Take care to wash your hands,

especially evry time you use the toilet.

Are there eny questions?"

___ ___ ___ ___

would, should, could

1 Look at each word below.
Say it out loud, cover it, then write it. Check your spelling.

would	should	could
_____	_____	_____

2 Colour in the box with the correct spelling in the passage below.

"I [would] [wood] like to watch *Frozen* tonight," said Pippa. "We [could] [cud] buy popcorn."

"[Should] [Shud] we ask Cal to join us?" said Mira. "It [wud] [would] be nice to see him. And he [could] [cud] bring the popcorn!"

3 Write two or three sentences using the words **could**, **should** and **would**. Here is an example:

I wish I **could** fly to the moon! I **would** see the stars and if I **should** fall, I **would** land on the fluffy clouds.

_____

_____

_____

Christmas, most, only, sugar, sure

1 Look at each word below.
Say it out loud, cover it, then write it. Check your spelling.
Remember to always write **Christmas** with a capital C!

Christmas	most	only
_____	_____	_____

sugar	sure
_____	_____

2 Write the missing words in the sentences below.
Remember to use a capital letter at the beginning of a sentence.

_____ is the _____ time of the year when I can be _____ all my family will get together.

If _____ it would stop raining! We have been stuck inside _____ of the day.

Last _____, Erin got the _____ beautiful chocolates, coated with _____ .

behind, find, kind, mind, wild, climb

1 Look at each word below.
Say it out loud, cover it, then write it. Check your spelling.

behind	find	kind
_____	_____	_____
mind	wild	climb
_____	_____	_____

2 Write the missing words in the two rhymes below.

I think you will _____ that if *you* are _____

People will smile and *they* will be _____.

As we start to _____, the wind is _____.

I hope you do not _____ if I fall _____.

3 Write a silly sentence using as many of these words as you can.
Here is an example:
The **wild**, **kind** boy wanted to **climb** up to the
clouds to **find** his **mind**, which he had left **behind**.

_____

_____

_____

_____

hour, door, floor, poor

1 Look at each word below.

Say it out loud, cover it, then write it. Check your spelling.

hour	door	floor	poor
____	____	____	____

2 Say the word **hour** out loud. What do you notice?

You don't sound the 'h'. Here, the 'h' is a **silent letter**.

Can you think of another word that sounds the same as **hour**?

our

3 Use the clues to fill in the crossword.

Across

1. You open me to enter a room.
2. You stand on me every day!

Down

3. Describes someone with no money.
4. A unit of time.

half, pass, grass, class

1 Look at each word below.
Say it out loud, cover it, then write it. Check your spelling.

half	pass	grass	class
___	___	___	___

2 Say the word **half** out loud. What do you notice?

You don't sound the 'l'. Here, the 'l' is a **silent letter**.

Now say the words **pass**, **grass** and **class** out loud.

What do you notice?

Can you think of any more words that rhyme with these words?

They rhyme!

3 Write the missing words in the sentences below.
Remember to use a capital letter at the beginning of a sentence.

_____ of my _____ likes maths.

We _____ our homework to the teacher.

In summer, we do handstands on the _____ .

4 Write a silly sentence using all four words.
Here is an example: Please **pass** the **grass** to **half** the **class**!

___
___
___

busy, after, path, bath

1 Look at each word below.

Say it out loud, cover it, then write it. Check your spelling.

busy	after	path	bath
_____	_____	_____	_____

2 Write the missing words in the passage below.

Remember to use a capital letter at the beginning of a sentence.

Dad is very _____. He is brushing the leaves

off the _____. _____ he has finished, he will

relax in a hot _____.

3 Use different colours to colour in the train carriages that spell the words **busy**, **after**, **path**, and **bath**. Find the letters to spell one word in each train.

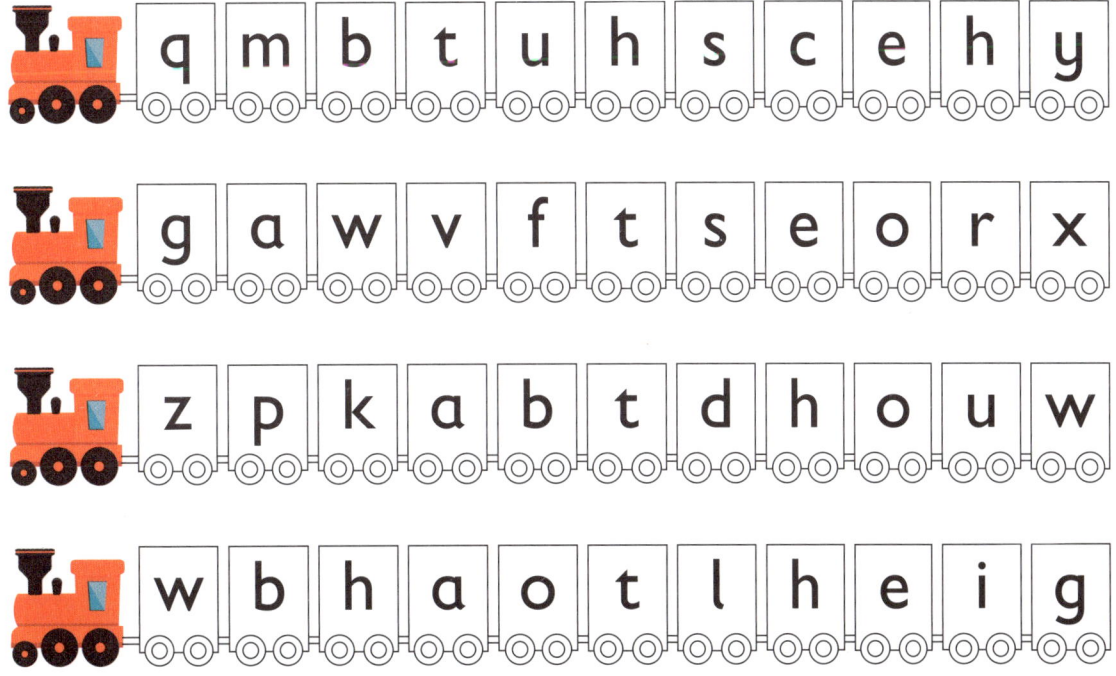

past, fast, last, plant

1 Look at each word below.
Say it out loud, cover it, then write it. Check your spelling.

past	fast	last	plant
_____	_____	_____	_____

2 Unscramble the jumbled words.

atsf _____   tsal _____

apst _____   tpnal _____

3 Write the missing words in this passage.

Tilly walks _____. She walks

_____ the first shop. She walks

_____ some more shops. Finally,

she walks to the _____ shop, where

she buys a _____ for her mum.

4 Now write a silly sentence using all four of these words.

_____
_____
_____
_____

water, beautiful, pretty

1 Look at each word below.

Say it out loud, cover it, then write it. Check your spelling.

water	beautiful	pretty
_____	_____	_____

2 Think of a way to help you spell the tricky part of the word **beautiful**.

b blue   **b**…
e elephants   **e**…
a are   **a**…
u unhappy   **u**…

3 Write the missing letters in the sentences below.

The b _____ f ___ butterfly lands on the

p _____ flower.

The _____ y flowers need ___ t ___ to

help them grow.

I like swimming in the _____ u _____ l blue

__ a _____ when I am on holiday.

break, steak, great

1 Look at each word below.

Say it out loud, cover it, then write it. Check your spelling.

break	steak	great
_____	_____	_____

2 Now say the words **break** and **steak** out loud. What do you notice?

3 Write the missing words in the rhyme.

My dad is _____ but he often works late.

When he has a _____, he likes to eat _____.

4 Find the words that have been spelled incorrectly and write the correct spellings on the lines below.

Sol ate a stake sandwich for lunch. At brake time, he played a grate game with his friend, Ben, to see who could throw the ball the furthest. "Don't brake the window!" yelled their teacher.

_____ _____ _____

Mr, Mrs, parents, people

1 Look at each word below.

Say it out loud, cover it, then write it. Check your spelling.

Mr	Mrs	parents	people
___	___	___	___

2 **Mr** and **Mrs** are funny spellings! We use **Mr** before the surname or full name of a man, and **Mrs** before the surname or full name of a married woman.

Think of the names of the different teachers in your school.

3 Think of a way to help you spell the tricky word **people**.

p	parrots	p…
e	enjoy	e…
o	opening	o…
p	pretty	p…
l	little	l…
e	envelopes	e…

4 Write the missing words in the sentences below.

_____ Ahmed drives his car to school.

_____ Smith rides her bike to work.

Leo's mummy and daddy

are his _____ .

Some _____ love fruit and vegetables.

money, who, whole

1 Look at each word below.

Say it out loud, cover it, then write it. Check your spelling.

money	who	whole
_____	_____	_____

2 What do you notice when you say the words **who** and **whole** out loud? You don't sound the 'w'. Here, the 'w' is a **silent letter**. Can you think of any more words that have a silent letter?

3 Use different colours to colour in the train carriages that spell the words **money**, **who** and **whole**. Find the letters to spell one word in each train.

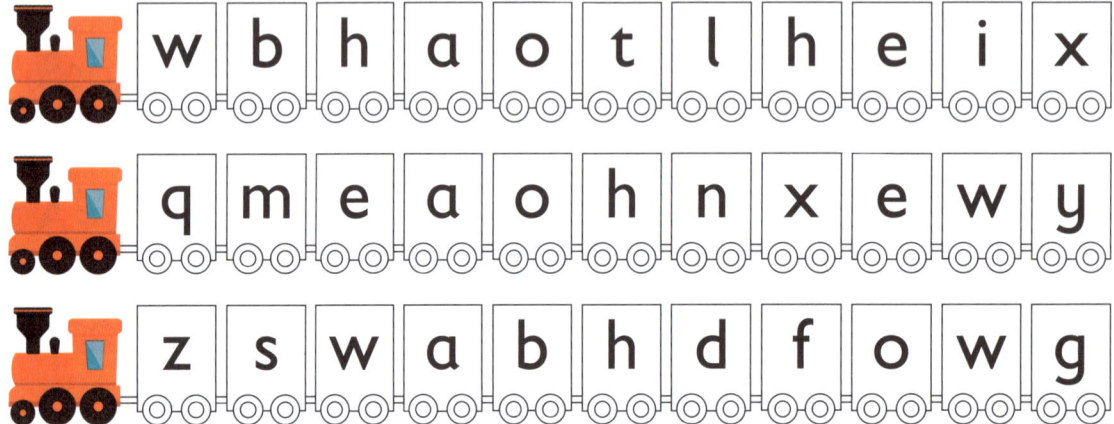

4 Fill in the missing words in the passage below.

The king, _____ lives in a big castle,

has more _____ than anyone in

the _____ world. He is very kind

and shares his _____ with

the _____ of his kingdom.

move, improve, prove

1 Look at each word below.

Say it out loud, cover it, then write it. Check your spelling.

move	improve	prove
_____	_____	_____

2 Use the clues to solve the crossword.

Across
1. Get better
2. Show that something is true

Down
3. Change position

3 Write the missing words in the sentences below.

Harriet's mum wants to _____ house.

Ted needs to _____ his spellings.

Faiz will _____ he didn't push Milly.

4 Make up a sentence using all three words.
Here is an example:
I need to **improve** my **moves** to **prove** that I am a good dancer!

_____

_____

_____

clothes, father, even, eye

1 Look at each word below.

Say it out loud, cover it, then write it. Check your spelling.

clothes	father	even	eye
_____	_____	_____	_____

2 Write the missing words in the passage below.

Remember to use a capital letter at the beginning of a sentence.

My _____ is taking me shopping for new

_____ . _____ if I don't see anything

that catches my _____ , I know we will have fun.

3 Use the clues to solve the riddles.

I am one of a pair. _____

I am the opposite of odd. _____

You like to wear me! _____

I am another word for dad. _____

4 Make up a silly sentence using the words. Here is an example:
My **father** likes to wear pirate **clothes** and **even** wears an **eye** patch!

_____

_____

_____

Answers

Page 4

3. I am Sofia. I go **to** school.
   I am Tom. I have **a** ball and **the** ball is red.
   My old ball **was** blue.

Page 5

3. **is**, **his**, **said** and **says** circled.

4. Dad **is** tired.
   The girl **says / said** hello.
   That is **his** ball.
   I **said** goodbye.

Page 6

3. **They**; **by**; **of**; **are**

Page 7

3.

4. **Once** upon a time, a cat lived on a farm. "Where is **my** food?" he asked **one** day. "I can't **do** any hunting if I haven't had **my** food!"

Page 8

3. These objects circled:

4. **She** likes **me**.
   He eats apples.
   We read our books.
   Be careful!

Page 9

3. After my breakfast, I feel **full**.
   I **push** my bike up the hill.
   We **put** the toys in the box.
   My baby brother likes to **pull** my hair.

4. push – rush; pull – dull; put – cut; full – gull
   (pull could be linked with gull and full linked with dull)

Page 10

3.

5. There is **no** <u>snow</u> left in the garden!
   Please can we **go** on the <u>slow</u> rides at the fair?
   The temperature is <u>low</u> **so** wear your warm coat.

Page 11

3. **chair**, **care**, **their**, **dare** and **fair** circled.

4. We shall meet **our** friends in one <u>hour</u>.
   Where is the <u>pear</u> that Mum gave me?
   Iris **has** <u>as</u> many crayons <u>as</u> I have.
   There is the <u>pair</u> of socks I was looking for!

Page 12

3. The book is over **here**.
   Today, after **school**, we are watching a film but yesterday, we **were** playing football.

4. rewe = were, yadot = today, loocsh = school, ehre = here

Page 13

3. house; friend; ask

4. Answers will vary. Example: I shall ask my friend to come to my house.

Page 14

2. love; some; come; some; love

3. Would you like to **come** with me
   To see the sea and swim with me?
   How I **love** to splash and run!
   Some day I hope you'll **come** with me!

Page 15

2. one **child**; two **children**

3. Answers will vary.

4. (word search with: because, again, child, children)

Page 16

2. A little **old** man and a little **old** woman lived in a little **old** house. One day, the little old woman found a **gold** coin. "**Hold** your hands out. I **told** you we would be rich!"
   "Now we **both** have enough money for fire wood," he said. "We will never be **cold** again!"

3. (crossword: 1across gold, 2down both, 3down cold, 4down hold)

Page 17

4. many; Everybody; every; any

Page 18

2. The following words coloured in: **would**; **could**; **Should**; **would**; **could**.

3. Answers will vary.

Page 19

2. **Christmas** is the **only** time of the year when I can be **sure** all my family will get together.
   If **only** it would stop raining! We have been stuck inside **most** of the day.
   Last **Christmas**, Erin got the **most** beautiful chocolates, coated with **sugar**.

Page 20

2. I think you will **find** that if *you* are **kind**
People will smile and *they* will be **kind**.

   As we start to **climb**, the wind is **wild**.
I hope you do not **mind** if I fall **behind**.

3. Answers will vary.

Page 21

3.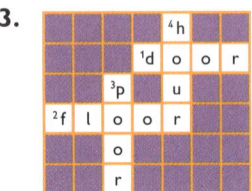

Page 22

3. **Half** of my **class** likes maths.
We **pass** our homework to the teacher.
In summer, we do handstands on the **grass**.

4. Answers will vary.

Page 23

2. Dad is very **busy**. He is brushing the leaves off the **path**. **After** he has finished, he will relax in a hot **bath**.

3. Letters coloured in as shown:

   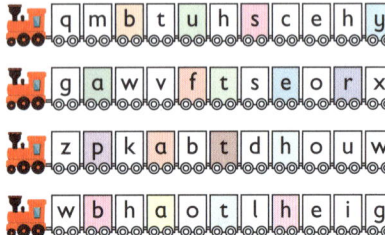

Page 24

2. atsf = fast; tsal = last; apst = past; tpnal = plant

3. Tilly walks **fast**. She walks **past** the first shop. She walks **past** some more shops. Finally, she walks to the **last** shop, where she buys a **plant** for her mum.

4. Answers will vary.

Page 25

3. The b**eau**ti**ful** butterfly lands on the p**re**tty flower.
The p**re**tty flowers need **wa**ter to help them grow.
I like swimming in the b**eau**ti**ful** blue **wa**ter when I am on holiday.

Page 26

3. My dad is **great** but he often works late.
When he has a **break**, he likes to eat **steak**.

4. steak; break; great; break

Page 27

4. **Mr** Ahmed drives his car to school.
Mrs Smith rides her bike to work.
Leo's mummy and daddy are his **parents**.
Some **people** love fruit and vegetables.

Page 28

3. Letters coloured in as shown:

   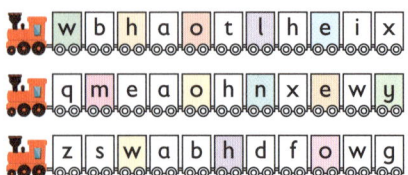

4. The king, **who** lives in a big castle, has more **money** than anyone in the **whole** world. He is very kind and shares his **money** with the **whole** of his kingdom.

Page 29

2.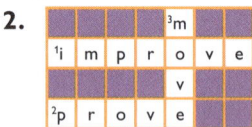

3. Harriet's mum wants to **move** house.
Ted needs to **improve** his spellings.
Faiz will **prove** he didn't push Milly.

4. Answers will vary.

Page 30

2. My **father** is taking me shopping for new **clothes**. **Even** if I don't see anything that catches my **eye**, I know we will have fun.

3. eye; even; clothes; father

4. Answers will vary.